LITTLE BOOK OF

JANE AUSTEN

LITTLE BOOK OF
JANE
AUSTEN

First published in the UK in 2006

© G2 Entertainment Limited 2014

www.G2ent.co.uk

Printed and bound in Europe

ISBN 978-1-909040-04-5

Contents

Introduction

Often revered as the first writer to give the novel its modern-day character, Jane Austen was widely read during her own lifetime, even though her books were published anonymously. With just six major titles – *Sense And Sensibility*, *Pride And Prejudice*, *Mansfield Park*, *Emma*, *Persuasion* and *Northanger Abbey* – Austen, who began her writing career in order to entertain her family, became one of the greatest classical authors in the English language.

Jane's father, the Reverend George Austen, was born in 1731. His mother died in childbirth and, when his father died a year after marrying for the second time, George was sent to live with his aunt in Tonbridge, Kent; his stepmother did not want the responsibility of her husband's offspring. The handsome young George Austen earned a fellowship to study at St John's College, Oxford, where he also worked as assistant chaplain and dean of arts. His time at the university saw him awarded Bachelor of Arts, Master of Arts and Bachelor of Divinity degrees, while he also worked as a lecturer in Greek.

The quiet, scholarly Austen met Cassandra Leigh, who was born in 1739, when she visited her uncle in Oxford. Documents written at the time confirm the Reverend Austen was devotedly in love with his witty and lively wife, who ran an economical yet comfortable household. The couple went on to have eight children (six sons and two daughters) who, unusually for the time, all survived into adulthood. It is known

Left: *An original family portrait of English novelist Jane Austen*

Right: *Steventon, the birthplace of Jane Austen*

from Jane's letters to her family that she enjoyed a happy childhood during which she was cared for lovingly.

Jane was the Austens' second daughter and the seventh of the eight children. James (1765-1819) was the oldest of the Austen siblings and, like his father, a scholarly type. He left for Oxford University at the age of 14 in 1779 and was ordained as a clergyman in 1787. George Austen (1766-1838), named after his father, suffered developmental disabilities and was possibly profoundly deaf. He was forced to live in care for his entire life.

Edward (1767-1852), who had a head for business, was adopted by Thomas and Catherine Knight, extremely rich cousins of the Austen family, in the early 1780s. He experienced the 'Grand Tour' – a custom of the time in which wealthy young men travelled around Europe – before inheriting his adoptive family's estate and taking on their family name. Henry Austen was born in 1771 and, like his mother, was witty and charismatic. Having become Jane's favourite brother despite his failed ventures (he was declared bankrupt in 1815), he died some 33 years after his famous younger sister.

The next child born to George and Cassandra was their first daughter, Cassandra Elizabeth (1773-1845), who was Jane's most constant companion and true confidante, a fact that is evident from the 100 or so surviving letters Jane wrote to her sister. Cassandra, however, destroyed many of the letters in the years following the young author's death.

Both Frank (1774-1865) and Charles (1779-1852) joined the Royal Navy when they reached the age of 12. Both were based in Portsmouth and went on to become admirals after fighting in the Napoleonic wars.

Born in Steventon, near Basingstoke, on 16 December 1775, Jane Austen spent the first 25 years of her life in Hampshire, mainly being tutored at home. She did, however, attend school occasionally and was fortunate to receive an education that was much broader than that of many of her peers.

Jane's aptitude for writing led to her entertaining her family with her musings and literature – both her parents were avid readers despite the fact that reading novels was considered a questionable activity at the time. Jane's earliest writings date from about 1787, when she was around 12 years old, but she was renowned for being reticent about revealing her work to the wider world. She wrote on small pieces of paper that she would hide quickly should visitors come to the rectory. Later in life, she let a creaking door remain unfixed so she could hear visitors approaching and have just enough time to hide her work.

Her early writings were observant and chatty and she was supported wholeheartedly by her parents, who encouraged their young daughter's aspirations. They bought Jane paper and a writing desk and even tried to help get her work published; *First Impressions* (later titled *Pride And Prejudice*) would be the first novel offered for publication.

As Jane grew and matured into a young woman she socialised with the upper middle classes and rich landed gentry, whom she went on to satirise in her novels. Her outlook was further broadened by the numerous relatives and friends with whom she spent her time. It became commonplace for the Austen family to put on amateur theatricals: between 1782 and 1784 the family put on plays at the Steventon rectory and three years later had advanced to more elaborate productions, mainly staged in a barn beside the family home.

Jane continued to read extensively and critically, and this led to her first juvenilia, which included comic and amusing pieces: parodies and variations of 18th century literature in both novel and serious history formats. By the age of 23 she had written three novels: *Elinor And Marianne*, an early version of *Sense And Sensibility* (1811); *First Impressions*, which was to see the light of day later as *Pride And Prejudice* (1813); and *Susan*, an early version of *Northanger Abbey* (1818). George Austen offered *First Impressions* to a publisher but the firm declined even to look at the manuscript.

With a fairly good income of around £600 a year, Rev Austen was nevertheless by

no means rich (he had eight children to support, after all), but his wife and children lived a comfortable existence. Their means were supplemented by the tutoring of pupils who came to live with the family while they were studying. In 1783, Cassandra and Jane were sent to Mrs Cawley in Oxford and later Southampton to further their education. An infectious disease at the school saw both girls brought home, and they then attended the Abbey boarding school in Reading. Back at home – where most of their tutoring took place – the two sisters were taught piano and drawing, but Rev Austen's extensive library of 500 books gave Jane the foundation she desired and satisfied her thirst for knowledge.

Her life consisted of learning and social events including dances and parties (which she particularly enjoyed), but she also loved visits to London, Bath and Southampton, where she would attend concerts and watch plays. Although she never married, she had a mutual flirtation with Thomas Lefroy, later to become Chief Justice of Ireland but at the time too impecunious to be able to marry Jane. He was a relative of Mrs Anne Lefroy, one of the author's close friends between 1795 and 1796. She wasn't particularly happy about the relationship and tried to interest Jane in Rev Samuel Blackall, but the young writer was less than impressed. She was even less impressed when her father decided to retire and take his family to Bath in late 1800.

The family, who moved in 1801, were in the habit of visiting the seaside for a family holiday every summer. It was on one of these holidays that Jane, 27 at the time, met a young suitor whom her sister Cassandra thought would be appropriate, but before the young couple could formalise their union the family were advised of his death. The only existing evidence that gives credence to this story is in the letters that Cassandra wrote to various nieces after Jane's death. It has been suggested that this experience might have influenced the plot of *Persuasion* (1817): Anne Elliot, the novel's heroine, is 27 when she experiences a disappointment in affairs of the heart.

This brief encounter was followed by a proposal from Harris Bigg-Wither, a 21-year-old son of the Bigg family of Manydown, near Steventon. Jane is known to have accepted the proposal even though she was not in love with Bigg-Wither, and she retracted her agreement the following day. Despite the fact that it caused some social

Above: *4 Sydney Place, the Bath residence of Jane Austen*

Left: *The Rice portrait of Jane Austen that has been the subject of debate and controversy*

Right: *The Royal Crescent in Bath, the height of fashion in Regency times*

embarrassment, Jane was adamant in her decision and returned as quickly as possible to her family in Bath.

When George Austen died in 1805 the family's income was reduced considerably, and Cassandra and her daughters – the only two remaining 'children' at home – had to rely on support from the Austen sons and a small sum of money left to young Cassandra by her fiancé Thomas Fowle, who had died of yellow fever in the Caribbean in 1797. Fowle had travelled overseas to take up a post as a military chaplain. He and Cassandra had been engaged for many years but had been unable to marry for lack of money. Rev Austen would not have had a great deal financially to give either of his daughters for marriage.

After a brief stay in Clifton in 1806, mother and daughters moved the same year to Southampton, where Jane wrote about her 'happy escape' from Bath. In Southampton the women were now closer to the two youngest sons, Frank and Charles, who were still based in Portsmouth, and they lived with Frank and his family. Then, in 1809, the family moved once again, this time to Chawton near Winchester, where the now wealthy Edward provided a cottage for his mother and sisters on one of his estates.

Having sold *Northanger Abbey* to a publisher before leaving Southampton, Jane resumed her quest for another publisher and revised *Sense And Sensibility*, which was accepted for publication in late 1810 or early 1811. It was published anonymously in 1811 – the author wrote under the pen name of 'A Lady' – and received fairly favourable reviews. The first edition eventually gave Jane a profit of £140.

Encouraged by the novel's success, she went on to revise *Pride And Prejudice* and sold the manuscript in 1812 for a flat fee of £110. Publication took place in January 1813 while the writing of *Mansfield Park* was well under way. The third novel was published in May 1814 following the second edition of *Sense And Sensibility*, which appeared in October 1813. The author was already hard at work on *Emma*, which was published

Above: *Chawton where her principal novels were written*

in December 1815 and was dedicated to the Prince Regent, the future King George IV. The following year, a second edition of *Mansfield Park* was published but failed to achieve the same sales level as the 1814 first edition. For 12 months from August 1815, Jane worked steadily on *Persuasion* and it was during this time that she began to suffer from ill health.

The author was particularly influenced by the likes of Henry Fielding (1707–1754), the English novelist and dramatist renowned for his earthy humour and satirical prowess. As well as being the author of the famous novel *Tom Jones*, the aristocratic Fielding was also the founder of the Bow Street Runners – the forerunner to London's 'Bobbies' and today's Metropolitan Police. Unlike Fielding, who was the first author to openly admit that his prose fiction was pure artefact and gave his characters little emotional depth, Austen bestowed great profundity on her characters.

She was also influenced by Fielding's rival and peer Samuel Richardson (1689–1761), who is best known for his novels *Pamela: Or, Virtue Rewarded* (1740), *Clarissa: Or, The History Of A Young Lady* (1748) and *Sir Charles Grandison* (1753). However, Richardson's writing was typical of his time in that he chose to 'hide' the fictional nature of his works by using the guise of 'letters' written by the protagonist, in order to give his prose more recognition and clout with the 18th century readership. But like Fielding and Austen later on, he was keen to explore the moralistic values of his time and *Pamela* had been a publishing sensation.

Another influence on Austen was Sir Walter Scott (1771–1832), the Scottish

Below: *Jane Austen was greatly influenced by Henry Fielding*

historical novelist and poet who enjoyed a prolific career on an international level with readerships in Europe, Australia and North America during his lifetime. Among his most famous works are *Ivanhoe, Rob Roy, The Lady Of The Lake* and *Waverley*. Austen's work was also influenced by Samuel Johnson, William Cowper, Fanny Burney and George Crabbe.

She was widely, if moderately, revered during her lifetime; some critics thought her novels too repetitive and overtly 'moral'. But the plots were well constructed and she received particular praise from Scott, who felt Austen's attention to detail and the depiction of the ordinary feelings of her characters was exquisite. Another fan was the Prince Regent, who instructed his librarian to give Jane a guided tour of his London library. The essayist Thomas Babington Macaulay and the poets Robert Southey and Samuel Taylor Coleridge were also ardent admirers of her work.

However, there was one literary giant that Austen failed to impress: the American writer Mark Twain, who said: 'Jane Austen? Why, I go so far as to say that any library is a good library that does not contain a volume by Jane Austen. Even if it contains no other book.' Despite the fact that Anne Brontë was often regarded as a writer with 'Jane Austen qualities', her sister Charlotte was also indifferent to her fellow writer and criticised the narrow scope of Austen's fiction. But other writers, including Rudyard Kipling, have been huge admirers. Kipling even wrote *The Janeites,* a short story about a group of soldiers who were ardent Austen fans.

Austen began work on *Sanditon* in early 1817 but gave up on the novel in March. April of that year saw the 41-year-old author write her will, by which she left most of what she had to her sister Cassandra. The latter moved Austen to rented rooms in Winchester for treatment for suspected Addison's disease, which occurs when the adrenal glands do not produce enough of the hormone cortisol (and, in some cases, the hormone aldosterone). Sometimes known as adrenal insufficiency, the disease can cause weight loss, muscle weakness, fatigue, low blood pressure and sometimes

Left: *Samuel Richardson's realism impressed the young Jane*

darkening of the skin. The disease was particularly common (although it was unnamed) during the 19th century as a complication of tuberculosis. In Austen's case it proved fatal and the author died in her sister's arms on Friday, 18 July 1817.

She was buried in the north aisle of Winchester Cathedral on July 24, with an interesting inscription on her gravestone that mentions the 'sweetness of her temper' and refers to her Christian humility. However, it is clear from both Austen's novels and her letters – particularly to Cassandra – that she was far more than a 'sweet' ordinary woman. The inscription also fails to mention the author's literary prowess, but this is perhaps not surprising considering that all her works were published anonymously and each advertised 'Written by A Lady' – something that was not uncommon at the time.

Her family mourned her deeply and their feelings were summed up in the words of a poem by James Austen:

In her, rare union, were combined a fair form,
And a fairer mind;
Hers fancy quick, and clear good sense,
And wit which never gave offence;
A heart as warm as ever beat,
A temper even; calm and sweet.

Though quick and keen her mental eye
Poor nature's foibles to espy,
And seemed forever on the watch,
Some trails of ridicule to catch
Yet not a word she ever penned
Which hurt the feelings of a friend.

Chapter 1

Austen Country

Nestling in a quiet spot between Basingstoke and Winchester lies the village of Steventon, birthplace and home to Jane Austen for more than half her life. A keen walker, she would often walk to Popham Lane, where she would collect the family post from a building known today as the Wheatsheaf Inn.

The family home, the 17th century, seven-bedroom rectory in Steventon, was repaired during the 1760s for the arrival of Rev Austen and his family. The Reverend was known to farm the fields surrounding his home, while his wife grew potatoes – quite an innovation at the time. Formal gardens with a turf walkway and a grassy bank marked the grounds and a driveway was built to receive carriages. The family performed their elaborate plays and comic theatricals for friends and relations in a barn situated in the grounds, but during the winter months the performances were moved into the more formal surroundings of the dining room. A private footpath of hedgerows and mixed shrubs was later cultivated to provide a pathway to the church, while chestnut trees, firs and elms adorned one side of the rectory.

Sadly, the building is no more. Much of the dilapidated property was demolished soon after the author's death, but the 12th century church where Jane worshipped with her family is virtually unchanged. It remains very much as it would have been during her father's time and later when her oldest brother, James, took over the parish from his father. The church now houses a bronze plaque dedicated to the author, and her

Left: *Despite its beauty, Jane never commented on Bath's architecture*

Right: *The Circus in Bath*

brother is buried in the churchyard.

When James Austen died, Henry became the rector at Steventon until he was replaced by William Knight (Edward's son) in 1822. Following his retirement from the military and then the banking world, after he faced bankruptcy, Henry Austen became a member of the clergy in 1816 and became perpetual curate at Bentley, near Alton, where he stayed until 1839.

As well as attending dances and social evenings at the Assembly Rooms in Basingstoke, Jane and Cassandra were invited to a number of dances held in nearby large houses. The Vyne on the outskirts of Basingstoke, now a National Trust property, is one such place, while Ibthorpe, north of Andover, was home to the Lloyd family (Mary Lloyd later became James Austen's second wife). After being tenants of the Austens, the Lloyd family moved to Ibthorpe in 1792. When Mrs Lloyd died in 1805 (the same year as Rev George Austen), Martha Lloyd, Mary's sister, moved to Bath to live with Cassandra and her two daughters and later travelled with the family to Southampton and eventually Chawton. Martha remained with the family for around 20 years.

When Jane's parents moved to Bath on her father's retirement in 1801, she was not best pleased at having to move from her childhood home in the country. There has been much speculation that Jane detested Bath, but some writers who have studied her life and works disagree, offering the suggestion that her first impressions were influenced by her dismay at leaving her rural home. There is some evidence in chronicles of her everyday life that even though the young author grew more accustomed to the crowds (and pavements) she still sometimes took refuge in the gardens and any other place that offered natural beauty and charm. She was clearly bothered that Bath was, in fact, not Steventon.

The city of Bath was preoccupied with material wealth at the beginning of the 19th century and Austen was forced to tolerate it. However, what is clear in her novels is

Above: *The Pump Room was part of the social heart of Bath in Austen's day*

that the city gave the writer an extended experience of the contemporary society she wanted to write about. What she did love about Bath, despite the fact that she disliked its urban lifestyle, was its openness to a myriad of ideas, sights, sounds and interpretations. Interestingly, she never commented on the wonder of the city's architecture, either in her letters or novels, even though the city was in its heyday and its golden stone buildings were in immaculate condition. She didn't mention the famous Roman Baths, the Circus, the most beautiful piece of civil design in the country, or the outstanding Royal Crescent. To Austen, a building was an indication of wealth rather than taste, and all biographies imply that Bath crushed her writing style and greatly discouraged her.

However, Nigel Nicholson, writing in *The Spectator* in December 2003, said he believed these notions were misguided. Austen was already discouraged by the time she arrived in Bath, he wrote, and the rejection of *Pride And Prejudice* greatly contributed to her lack of writing before the move – and she had attempted nothing new for two years. He also stated that Austen's letters to Cassandra proved she was becoming reconciled to the move and was ready for a change of scene. She was bored with the social circles of Basingstoke and, her brothers having moved away from home to follow their respective careers, there was nothing much left for the remainder of the family in Steventon.

Nicholson also suggested that as a family, while living at 4 Sydney Place, opposite Sydney Gardens, the Austens enjoyed a far wider immersion in politics, religion, literature and discussions about the Napoleonic Wars than Jane's letters and novels suggested. He argued that the family enjoyed their life in their Georgian home, and suggested that with Austen's desire for new experiences and 'playful disposition', it was 'difficult to imagine her moping at home'.

After five years, and the death of her father, Jane, her mother, sister and Martha Lloyd were set to move again. This time the upheaval took them to the rented lodgings of Naval Captain Frank Austen and his family in Southampton. Frank and Mary Austen's first child (they would go on to have 11 in total) was on the way and the lodgings proved expensive for the family, so they all moved to an old-fashioned house in Castle Square, rented from the Marquess of Lansdowne. The garden ran along Southampton's old city walls, which overlooked the river, and the family had access to a promenade that ran the length of the walls.

Above: *Jane Austen's house is now a museum*

During the early 19th century, Southampton still had the aspect of a medieval town and the house would have looked westwards across the beautiful Southampton Water. Family excursions included trips on the River Itchen to Netley Abbey, and Jane, who had a love of walking, was known to have strolled along the banks of the Itchen and Test rivers and beside Southampton Water, as well as in the surrounding countryside. She and Cassandra continued to attend dances, some of which were held at the Dolphin Hotel (still in existence today), but financial constraints hampered their socialising to some degree. Visits to the New Forest were a firm favourite with the Austen family, who enjoyed seeing the outstanding scenery and famous wild ponies. They travelled the Beaulieu River and visited Beaulieu Abbey and the famous shipbuilding yards at Bucklers Hard.

Cassandra had intended the move to Southampton to be merely temporary, and after three years she moved her two daughters and their house guest Martha Lloyd to Chawton, near Alton, where they set up home in the former bailiff's house on the

Chawton estate. It was here that Jane found her true 'literary home' where she wrote on a small round table in the parlour. Her life was somewhat quieter at Chawton, and she resumed her career in a home surrounded by old varieties of flowers and herbs in a pretty garden.

Despite taking up writing again, she would walk each day with Cassandra, and they also went shopping in nearby Alton. The area was steeped in history: the village's earliest records appear in the Domesday survey of 1086. The present Chawton House was built during the time of the Armada (1588) and was eventually passed down to Elizabeth Knight (who had two husbands who were both required to change their surname to Knight).

Today, Jane Austen's House Museum, as Chawton cottage is known, is open to the public and receives 30,000 visitors a year. Austen regularly visited her niece, Anna Lefroy, the oldest daughter of her brother James and his first wife, Ann Mathew. Anna's memoirs about both her aunts, Cassandra and Jane, provide a great deal of information about the writer.

The bodies of both Cassandra Austen senior and her daughter Cassandra are buried at St Nicholas's Church, a short distance from Chawton. The church itself was destroyed by fire some time later and was rebuilt in 1872. Chawton House was restored in order to establish a Centre for the Study of Early English Women's Writing 1600–1830, and now houses more than 9,000 volumes and related manuscripts in its renowned library.

Below: *The Winchester house in which Jane Austen lived her final days*

Chapter 2

The Novels

Jane Austen is noted for her meticulous attention to detail and witty observations about early 19th century English society. Combining romantic comedy with social satire and psychological insight, she confidently portrays the quiet, day-to-day lives of members of the upper middle classes.

Her novels generally consist of two themes: loss of illusion (which challenges her main characters to adopt a more mature outlook) and the struggle between traditional moral ideals and how to reconcile these with the demands of everyday life. Many of the novels include as a feature characters learning by their mistakes, with Austen's insight into human nature showing her exceptional skill for a well thought out psychological approach. It was these strengths that led to the author becoming classed as one of the greatest novelists (and creator of the modern-day novel) of the 19th and 20th centuries.

Right: *Emma Thompson and Hugh Grant on the set of Sense and Sensibility*

Sense And Sensibility (1811)

Although not Austen's first novel, *Sense And Sensibility* was her first published work. Originally titled *Elinor And Marianne*, the book was revisited by Jane and submitted to Thomas Egerton in London for publication under its new name, with the first edition appearing in 1811. As its original title would suggest, the plot centres around two sisters, 19-year-old Elinor (the heroine, known for her sense) and 17-year-old Marianne (renowned for her sensibility, or emotion).

When the sisters' father, Henry Dashwood, dies leaving the family home at Norland and all his money to his first wife's son, John, his second wife and three daughters, Elinor, Marianne and 13-year-old Margaret, are left with no permanent home and little income. Their plight is largely brought about by John's wife, Fanny Dashwood (sister to Edward and Robert Ferrars), who with her manipulative and scheming ways persuades her husband to leave the four women virtually penniless. For his part, John Dashwood seems unconcerned with the situation in which he leaves his stepmother and three half-sisters. As a result, they are invited to stay with distant relatives, the Middletons, at Barton Park in Barton Cottage.

For Elinor, the move is a sad one due to her recent blossoming relationship with Edward Ferrars, the brother-in-law of John Dashwood. But life at Barton Park provides the sisters with new experiences and many new acquaintances, including retired officer and confirmed bachelor Colonel Brandon and the impetuous John Willoughby. When Marianne twists her ankle running down a hill in the rain she is rescued by the gallant Willoughby and from then on he courts her openly. The two are unabashed in their affections and deliberately flaunt their attachment. Willoughby leaves a miserable and lovesick Marianne at Barton Park when he suddenly announces that he must leave at once for business in London.

Two recently discovered relatives of Lady Middleton's mother, Mrs Jennings, arrive

at Barton Park as additional house guests. Anne and Lucy Steele do not bring good fortune for Elinor, as Lucy admits that she has secretly been engaged to Mr Ferrars for a year. At first Elinor assumes Lucy means Edward's younger brother Robert, but is shocked and heartbroken to learn that she means her own love, Edward.

Mrs Jennings invites Elinor and Marianne to stay with her in London, where the older sister learns from Colonel Brandon that there is news of the engagement between Willoughby and Marianne. However, this is a revelation to her family. Meanwhile, the well-intentioned Mrs Jennings is trying to marry off the two sisters as quickly as possible.

Marianne is particularly excited to meet Willoughby at a party, but he cruelly rejects his former love. She is further hurt by a letter she receives not long after, in which Willoughby denies that he ever had any feelings for her.

Some insight into this state of affairs is given to Elinor by Colonel Brandon, who confirms that Willoughby has in the past treated other young women the same way. His callousness is confirmed by Mrs Jennings, who also says that having squandered his fortune, the debauched young man has become engaged to a wealthy heiress, Miss Sophia Grey.

When Anne Steele lets slip that her younger sister is secretly engaged to Edward Ferrars, his mother is outraged and promptly disinherits him, and the family fortune is promised to Robert. Meanwhile, Elinor and Marianne visit friends (the Palmer family) in Cleveland on their return trip from London. Here, Marianne develops a severe cold – having taken many long walks in the rain – and she becomes gravely ill. On hearing of Marianne's plight, Willoughby decides to visit seeking forgiveness for his uncaring behaviour and offering an explanation for his ill-mannered treatment of her.

Elinor takes pity on the hapless young man and shares his story with her sister. However, Marianne realises, while she returns slowly to health, that she would never have been happy with Willoughby. Her mother and Colonel Brandon arrive at Cleveland and are relieved to find a convalescing Marianne. The family eventually return to Barton Park, where they learn that Lucy Steele and Mr Ferrars are engaged and wrongly assume that the groom-to-be is indeed Edward.

However, his arrival at Barton Park serves to confirm that money-grabbing Lucy Steele is in fact engaged to Robert Ferrars now that he will inherit from his mother. It allows Edward the chance to finally propose to Elinor while Colonel Brandon seeks Marianne's hand in marriage. The retired officer fell in love with Marianne early in the story and was always kind, honourable and gracious in his dealings with the family. While Mrs Dashwood and Margaret remain at Barton Cottage, the two couples live together, close by at Delaford.

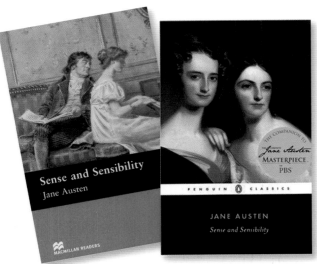

Sense and sensibility are commonly analysed by the author throughout and the distinction between the two is clearly symbolised by the characters of Elinor and Marianne Dashwood. Elinor demonstrates reason, restraint, social responsibility and all the qualities that adhere to 'sense' with her clear-headed concern for the welfare of others.

In contrast, Marianne represents emotion, spontaneity, devotion and impulsiveness, which are evident in her relationship with John Willoughby and which she openly and unashamedly flaunts; Elinor, meanwhile, is more discreet about her feelings for Edward Ferrars. The sisters represent completely differing temperaments throughout the novel in their attitudes to love and how they express their feelings.

Above & Right:
Sense and Sensiblity has been published many times over the years and is an international favourite

As an author, Austen did not fit neatly into any particular writing era. She was too early to be Victorian and a little too late to belong to the Regency era, and this shows in the cultural and historical resonances through the dichotomy between 'sense' and 'sensibility' and the fact that Austen was writing in the middle of two cultural movements: Classicism and Romanticism.

Elinor Dashwood represents 18th century neo-classicism and the author uses this character to allude to propriety, economic practicalities and perspective. However, the novel was just beginning to develop as a literary genre and Marianne leads towards the 'cult of sensibility' that was threatening to emerge representing romance, imagination, idealism and excess. The novel reminds the reader that the literary landscape was changing at that time. Austen was keen to emphasise that a woman's social standing was improved (quite literally) by marriage and her novels ultimately lead to the marriage of the heroine. The Dashwood sisters were no exception.

But *Sense And Sensibility* wasn't that straightforward. Indeed, Elinor did not lack passion, and Marianne was not always foolish and headstrong. What Austen did with the characters was to use their fundamental characteristics as starting points for dialogue. The happiness that the formerly impoverished sisters find towards the end of the novel comes about as a result of their willingness to learn from each other and their life experiences.

Perhaps Austen was trying to teach readers, through her wit and observations, that this was what life was actually about. Neither sense nor sensibility prevails; the author provides a logical balance between the two. This led to some criticism that the ending was disappointing, especially as Marianne marries a man whom she had not thought she could love. But the comic and subtle ironies used to describe characters such as the Middletons, Lucy Steele and Mrs Jennings have helped to persuade readers, both past and present, that *Sense And Sensibility* is Austen at her best.

Pride And Prejudice (1813)

Publishing *Pride And Prejudice* under the pen name of 'A Lady' may not have given Jane Austen the recognition she deserved for her work, but it did serve to provide her with anonymity at a time when the repressive atmosphere of English society likened a woman's presence in public life to a form of degradation. She was a realist who poked fun at the snobbishness of the gentry and sometimes the poor breeding of those lower down the social scale, but Austen depicted social advancement and the appropriate behaviour for each gender throughout her novels in an expert manner. Young men, for example, were advanced by their entry into the military or the church or through birth, while young women would find a firm social footing if they acquired wealth, i.e. through marriage. This novel was no exception. In fact, the opening sentence sums up the subject matter right from the start: 'It is a truth universally acknowledged, that a man in possession of a good fortune must be in want of a wife.'

At the start of the novel the young and extremely wealthy Charles Bingley rents Netherfield Park, a manor house, which causes a stir in the neighbouring village of Longbourn. It causes a particular sensation in the Bennet household, where five unmarried daughters – Jane, Elizabeth, Mary, Kitty and Lydia – are all desperately seeking a future husband. However, Mr Bennet, with his modest income, does not have a great deal of wealth to share between five daughters and their potential nuptials. The nosy and irrepressible Mrs Bennet has but one goal in life: to marry off her daughters. But her poor background and sometimes less than acceptable social behaviour often put off any potential suitors for her daughters.

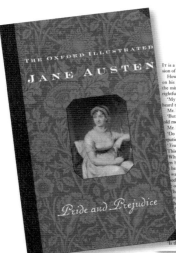

Above & Right:
Pride and Prejudice, the novel

Mr Bennet pays a social visit to Mr Bingley and the family are invited to attend a ball at which Charles will be present. Charles is immediately taken with Jane Bennet and spends much of the evening dancing with her while his close friend Fitzwilliam Darcy is disenchanted with the proceedings and flatly refuses to dance with Elizabeth (Mr Bennet's most loved daughter), whom he describes as uninteresting. His stubbornness to accept those with lower social standing than himself causes the guests at the ball to view Darcy as arrogant and obnoxious.

Over the course of the social calendar, however, he finds himself drawn to Elizabeth's intelligence and charm. The relationship between Jane and Charles continues to blossom and she decides to visit him at home. Caught in a torrential downpour on the way to Netherfield Park, Jane becomes ill and is forced to remain at the manor house for several days. Elizabeth finds herself wading through muddy fields to take care of her older sister and arrives bedraggled and mud-spattered, much to the disdain of Charles's sister, the snobbish Miss Bingley. She is further spited when she discovers that Darcy, whom she herself has her eye on, is quite taken with Elizabeth.

When Jane is well enough to return home, she and Elizabeth find Mr Collins, a pompous and snobbish clergyman, visiting their father. He is the heir to the Bennet family home (as an entailed property the house can only be passed to male relatives) and he quickly makes a proposal of marriage to Elizabeth. His pride is severely wounded when he is rejected but meanwhile, the Bennet sisters have made acquaintances with military officers based in a nearby town. One particular officer, George Wickham, strikes up a friendship with Elizabeth and explains to her that Darcy once cruelly cheated him out of his inheritance.

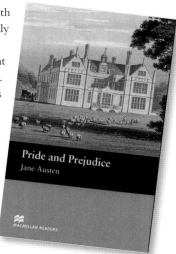

During the winter, Jane is dismayed to learn that Charles, his sister and Darcy have returned to London. Mr Collins becomes engaged to Charlotte Lucas (Elizabeth's closest friend) and the family are shocked that the daughter of a local knight is marrying for financial security. The marriage, however, goes ahead and Elizabeth promises to visit her friend in her new home.

Jane makes the journey to London to visit friends of her own and is disappointed when Charles makes no effort to visit her. She does, however, receive his sister, who is less than gracious. It seems that Mrs Bennet's endeavours to find suitable matches

Above:
*Groombridge
Place, Kent – the
Bennet home
in the 2005 film
adaptation of Pride
& Prejudice*

for her daughters may have been in vain. Unknown to the Bennets, however, Darcy is more and more taken with Elizabeth while Miss Bingley tries extremely hard to gain his attention. The fact that Elizabeth is not openly pursuing him in the same way as her rival makes her all the more endearing.

In the spring, Elizabeth keeps her promise to Charlotte and visits her friend who lives close to Lady Catherine de Bourgh. The latter happens to be Mr Collins's patron as well as Darcy's aunt. Here the two meet again and from then on Darcy begins to visit Mr Collins and Charlotte fairly regularly. But his unexpected and shocking marriage proposal is quickly rejected by Elizabeth and she tells her suitor he is rude and unpleasant and that she does not agree with his manipulative keeping of Charles Bingley away from Jane. She also scolds him for cheating Wickham out of his inheritance.

Following their disagreement, Darcy writes to Elizabeth and explains that he did indeed advise Bingley to distance himself from Jane, but not because the couple might not be suited; he claims he thought the relationship might not be serious enough. He also explains that Wickham is a liar and that the real reason they fell out was because the young officer had attempted to elope with Darcy's shy younger sister, Georgiana. Elizabeth finds herself re-evaluating her feelings for the man she once thought arrogant and obnoxious and on her return home is cold towards her former friend, George Wickham.

The younger Bennet sisters are rather heartbroken when they find out the military officers are to be stationed elsewhere, and Lydia persuades her father to let her spend the summer in Brighton – home of their new barracks – with an old colonel and friend of the family. In June, Elizabeth travels north with the Gardiner family (distant relatives) and arrives in Pemberley, near Darcy's estate. Having made sure that he is not at home, Elizabeth visits the estate and is very taken with the marvellous house and grounds. She also hears from Darcy's servants that he is a kind and generous master. Darcy makes a sudden appearance and invites Elizabeth and the Gardiners to stay. He also wishes to introduce Elizabeth to his sister, Georgiana.

Lydia and Wickham, meanwhile, elope and the news from home suggests that the young couple are living out of wedlock. Worried by the disgrace it would surely bring on her family, Elizabeth hurries home and her father, aided by Mr Gardiner, sets out to find Lydia. The search proves futile and the family are in despair. However, Mr Gardiner eventually finds the couple and writes to the Bennet household to say that

Wickham has agreed to marry Lydia in return for an annual income.

The entire family are convinced that Gardiner has paid Wickham off, but it comes to light that it is in fact Darcy who is maintaining the officer and his wife. Darcy has brought the Bennet family salvation. The newlyweds arrive in Longbourn and stay briefly. Mr Bennet is cold towards his daughter and son-in-law before they depart for Wickham's new assignment in the north of England.

Meanwhile, Charles Bingley returns to his rented manor house and resumes his courtship of Jane Bennet. Darcy returns also and often visits the Bennets, but makes no reference to his earlier proposal or his earlier desire to marry Elizabeth. Everyone is delighted when Charles proposes to Jane, however – all, that is, except his cold, calculating sister, Miss Bingley.

Lady Catherine then decides to visit Longbourn, where she takes Elizabeth to one side and tells the young woman of Darcy's intention to marry her. But Lady Catherine considers them an unsuitable match and insists that Elizabeth refuse her nephew's proposal. Elizabeth confirms she is not engaged to Darcy but refuses to answer anything that will affect her own happiness. While out walking with Darcy she accepts his second proposal. As is customary, Austen's heroines are married and find their much sought-after social standing.

This much-cherished love story is as popular today as it was in Austen's own time. As with all good stories, it takes the couple in question through a labyrinth of trials and tribulations before they can be united and the story can result in ultimate happiness. Initially, Elizabeth judges Darcy on her first impression through pride, while Darcy, for his part, judges Elizabeth through his own prejudice of her poorer social standing. With interference from Lady Catherine, snobbery from Miss Bingley and idiocy from Mrs Bennet, it seems as if true love will be lost in the anxieties of social connections, but the truth overcomes these obstacles and conquers in the end.

But, ever the realist, Austen also uses the character of Charlotte (and her marriage

Left: *Film scene from the 1940 adaption of the book, starring Greer Garson and Laurence Olivier*

to Mr Collins) to show that sometimes the head rather than the heart dictates fate and that sometimes it is financial security that may be the conqueror.

The novel shows just how important it is for a woman to ensure her reputation and that women are expected to behave in certain ways. Reputation is shown as of vital importance when Lydia elopes with Wickham and lives out of wedlock.

One of the main symbols or motifs of the novel is that of journeys. Each journey undertaken by the characters, however short, functions as a catalyst for change. Perhaps Austen was seeking changes in social structures and their interference in everyday lives, or perhaps she was merely accepting of the inevitable lack of change that society experienced at that time.

Mansfield Park (1814)

Appearing in print in 1814, *Mansfield Park* was written between 1811 and 1813. As is usual in a novel by Austen, there is much about social standing, but *Mansfield Park* goes further than any of her other titles in its social awareness. Here, Jane focuses on the slave trade and the roots of the British aristocracy's corruption and exploitation of others, helping to make *Mansfield Park* one of the author's least romantic works.

Young Fanny Price is sent to live with her wealthy relatives, Sir Thomas and Lady Bertram. Her mother, unlike her sister, Lady Bertram, married beneath her and Fanny's family are fairly poor and live in quite squalid surroundings. Her father, a disabled sailor, drinks heavily, but life is not a bed of roses for Fanny at Mansfield Park either. There she is consistently abused by another of her aunts, Mrs Norris, who runs the Bertrams' estate.

Fanny finds a friend in Edmund Bertram, who is planning to join the clergy while his older brother, Tom, is a drunk and his sisters, Maria and Julia, are more intent on marrying well and perpetuating their fashionable status than anything else. Fanny lives in a repressive environment and becomes shy and deferential.

While Sir Thomas is away in Antigua attending to his plantations, Henry and Mary Crawford (the brother and sister of the local minister's wife) arrive and with their cheerful and witty dispositions soon become an integral part of the Mansfield set. Henry flirts openly with Maria, who by now is engaged to the wealthy but boring Rushworth. The latter provides comic relief throughout the novel with his idiotic comments. When it suits him, Henry is also prone to flirting with Julia, but his sister Mary is initially only interested in Tom. However, she begins to find him boring and uninterested in her, so she finds herself increasingly attracted to Edmund. But she doesn't want to marry a clergyman and Fanny (although she doesn't want to admit it to herself) has quietly fallen in love with the younger brother.

Tom's friend, Yates, soon comes to visit and suggests that the party put on a play. The idea is eagerly received by everyone except Edmund and Fanny, who are both horrified by the suggestion that they should act. The play goes ahead despite their protestations (Edmund even has to play a part) and some racy scenes are acted out. Fanny is pressurised to step in at the last moment and is virtually forced to concede against her wishes, but Sir Thomas arrives home suddenly from his plantations. He is not best pleased with the play and quickly puts a stop to the nonsense, as he calls it.

When Henry fails to declare his love, Maria is married to Rushworth and she and Julia set out for London. Edmund, meanwhile, almost proposes to Mary on a number of occasions, but her cynical thoughts over his becoming a member of the clergy change his mind at the last moment. Edmund confides in Fanny, who is upset by his revelations, but she is being wooed (as a source of amusement) by Henry, who surprises himself by finding he is actually in love with her.

Meanwhile, Fanny has become indispensable as far as her uncle and aunt are concerned and when her brother William arrives they give a ball in her honour. Henry then helps William gain promotion in the navy and, using this as leverage, proposes to Fanny, who refuses him. Sir Thomas is upset by his niece's refusal of a wealthy man and as a punishment Fanny is sent home.

Edmund is ordained and continues to ponder his feelings for Mary, much to Fanny's

dismay. Henry refuses to give up on Fanny and while he's away on business, Mary writes to her to encourage her to accept her brother's proposal. Fate takes a hand when a series of unexpected events happen in rapid succession. Tom falls dangerously ill (a result of his constant partying) and Henry's business trip turns out to be his excuse for escaping and eloping with the married Maria. Julia, in a knee-jerk reaction, elopes with Yates and Fanny is requested back at Mansfield.

She arrives with her younger sister, Susan, and finds that Edmund has finally seen through Mary. She had openly wished Tom's illness would kill him so that Edmund would inherit. At this news Edmund turns to Fanny for consolation. While Henry and Maria's relationship doesn't last – she moves to the Continent with Mrs Norris – Julia and Yates are eventually reconciled to the family and Edmund finally marries Fanny. Susan takes up her sister's role within the Bertram household and all is well again.

The novel's plot is extremely complicated even though the crux is simple enough: the lead character's quest to find social status, which she does eventually through marriage to Edmund. With no way in which to have a professional life, Fanny's only option is to marry for security and status. The novel hails virtue and those characters who show promise are destined for an agreeable fate, while those who act inappropriately or selfishly are not.

What is clear is that Austen is questioning whether people can change. Certainly, Sir Thomas and Edmund seem to have learned from their experiences, but Maria, Mary and Henry appear to have learned nothing. Using both the city and rural life as a backdrop to events, Austen appears to be implying that the town provides a life of vice while the country teaches all that is good. However, she complicates things by portraying rural characters with faults and town characters with healthy reputations.

Austen's sexual awareness is particularly acute in this book, despite the fact that it would probably have been rather too direct in its approach during the early 19th century. Perhaps it is this that led to *Mansfield Park* becoming one of Austen's most controversial and least popular works. However, there is a great deal of satire in the novel and it is probably the most socially realistic of all.

Emma (1815)

Austen began writing Emma in January 1814 and finished it just over a year later, in March 1815. Published in three volumes, it was the fourth and last novel that Jane would see in print during her lifetime. An initial print run saw 2,000 copies readied for sale, but more than a quarter remained unsold at the end of the four years that followed. The profits for Austen were paltry. She earned less than £40 from the book before her death a year and a half after publication.

Written in a comic tone, the novel tells the story of Emma Woodhouse, who like all other Austen heroines finds her destiny in marriage. However, at the start of the story, Emma is convinced that despite being, in her own view, a natural at making good love matches, she will never marry. Having gained a modicum of success in bringing her governess, Miss Taylor, together with Mr Weston, a widower, Emma decides to act as matchmaker for her newly acquired friend, Harriet Smith. Despite the fact that Harriet's parentage is unknown, Emma decides that she should ultimately be a gentleman's wife and sets about trying to pair her with the village rector, Mr Elton.

However, Harriet is taken with Robert Martin, a wealthy farmer, and Emma advises her friend to reject his proposal. Harriet quickly becomes infatuated with Elton; he, however, is more interested in Emma and her matchmaking plans go awry.

Emma has one critic, her friend and brother-in-law Mr George Knightley, who watches her matchmaking efforts with cynicism and believes that Harriet and Robert Martin would be well suited to one another. With Harriet's lack of knowledge about her past, he also believes that she would be lucky to marry Martin. Meanwhile, Elton who has been rejected by Emma and offended at the suggestion that Harriet could

Above: *Emma, from which Austen earned less than £40*

Right: *A scene from Jane Austen's novel Emma*

possibly be his equal, leaves the village of Highbury and arrives in Bath, where he marries a young woman almost immediately.

Comforting an upset Harriet, who has become something of a victim of her friend's meddling, Emma is left pondering the question of who Frank Churchill is. Churchill is, in fact, the son of Mr Weston and was brought up by his aunt and uncle in London when his mother died. He has obviously come to visit his father and his new wife in Highbury and would have come sooner had it not been for his aunt's many illnesses and complaints.

Knightley is immediately suspicious of the young man, who is heir to the Churchill estates, and his feelings are compounded when Frank takes off for London merely to have a haircut. However, Emma, despite knowing nothing about Churchill, is very taken with him and can't help but notice that most of his charm is aimed directly at her. The heroine finds herself flattered by Frank's attentions and engages in mild flirtation with him but she is less enthusiastic about the arrival of Jane Fairfax, a beautiful and accomplished young woman of whom Emma is jealous.

Knightley is keen to support Jane and

EMMA.

There was no being displeased with such an encourager; for his admiration made him discern a likeness before it was possible.

defends her from Emma, claiming she deserves compassion. Unlike Emma, Jane will have to work as a governess in order to give herself some standing in the community and, as is often the case in Austen novels, suspicion, misunderstandings and intrigue ensue. Mrs Weston suspects that Knightley is keen to involve himself with Jane romantically, but Emma cannot entertain the idea.

Tiring of Frank, Emma dismisses him from her mind as a potential suitor and believes he would be better suited to Harriet. Meanwhile, everyone else assumes that Emma and Frank are forming a close attachment. Soon comes the village ball and Knightley gallantly offers to dance with Harriet, who has just been completely humiliated by Elton and his new wife.

The following day, Harriet is rescued once again when Frank saves her from gypsy beggars and she tells Emma that she has fallen in love with a man above her social station.

Above: *Colour illustration depicting a scene from Jane Austen's novel Emma*

Emma wrongly assumes that Harriet is talking about Frank and laughs at Knightley's suggestion that Jane and Frank may have a secret understanding.

At a picnic attended by Jane's aunt, Miss Bates – herself a kindly soul – Emma is less than kind to Jane's kin and openly flirts with Frank, an action for which she is pulled up short by Knightley. At the loss of her brother-in-law's approval Emma is reduced to tears.

News then arrives that Frank's frail aunt in London has died. But the news doesn't just affect Frank; it brings about an unexpected revelation that slowly begins to unravel all the suspicion and intrigue that abounded in the community of Highbury. It transpires that Frank and Jane are secretly engaged and that his attentions towards Emma were a cover for his true feelings.

With his uncle's approval, Frank is now free to marry Jane and Emma worries that Harriet will, once again, be humiliated. But Harriet surprises her friend by revealing that she is in love with Knightley – not Frank – and she strongly believes that her feelings are reciprocated. But the news does not bring happiness for the heroine, who has to admit to herself that she too is in love with Knightley. Emma is placated when Knightley declares his love for her and Harriet is saved further upset and humiliation when Robert Martin proposes to her for a second time. The novel ends with two weddings and the answer to the question of who loves whom.

Austen was wrongly convinced that, as the author, she would be one of few people who would like the character of Emma. She warns the reader that, with her handsome looks and comfortable life, her heroine is quite used to her own way and thinks 'a little too much of herself'. But by using a narrator who comfortably slips between narrating the story and relating things from Emma's point of view, Austen is not clear about how harsh she wishes her readers to be in their opinions of Emma and, although the narration is quite complicated, she can leave the reader feeling both sympathetic with and frustrated by the main character.

Persuasion (published posthumously, 1818)

Although her health was failing, Austen wrote *Persuasion* in less than a year. But it would be another year after her death before the fifth manuscript would make it into print, published by John Murray. The book made a tidy profit of £500, which doesn't seem much by today's standards but was more money than Austen would have seen in her lifetime.

Representing a mature style of writing, more so than any of the previous novels, the book is an exciting, comic yet satirical story, once again aimed at the echelons of the titled upper classes. However, Austen does reflect the esteem in which she, and society in general, held the British Navy as the defender of the British Empire. The navy heroes in the novel serve to introduce her ideal of rougher manliness than the genteel landed gentry whom she so convincingly portrayed in the four earlier works, and *Northanger Abbey*, which was published in a bound volume with *Persuasion*.

At 27, the protagonist, Anne Elliot, is no longer considered youthful. This was a first for Austen and perhaps described her own feelings. However, the novel was also innovative in that it discussed the worth of the self-made man, in particular Captain Frederick Wentworth. Austen was keen to discuss the worthiness of men who reached the upper strata of society through their own initiative and not just because they were born to such standing.

The novel opens with a brief historical background to the respected, titled landowners the Elliots. Lady Elliot had died 14 years previously and Sir Walter was left bringing up three daughters: Elizabeth and Anne, who are single, and Mary, the youngest who is married to wealthy Charles Musgrove. Sir Walter has growing debts brought about by his lavish spending but when family friend Lady Russell, who acts as a mother figure in place of the late Lady Elliot, suggests that he curb his overspending he is mortified to learn that reducing his outgoings would mean giving up his comforts.

As a vain man, Sir Walter is horrified, but faces no other option so the family relocate to Bath, where living expenses will be more manageable.

Their former home, Kellynch Hall, the family estate, is promptly rented to Admiral and Mrs Croft, an exceptionally wealthy couple. Sir Walter is prejudiced in his belief that the navy can propel ordinary men into positions of distinction, but he is satisfied that Admiral Croft is a suitable tenant. Incidentally, Anne Elliot is desperately in love with Mrs Croft's brother. Anne was engaged to him eight years before, but was

persuaded to call off the union by Lady Russell, who did not deem the young man suitable by nature of his more lowly birth. By meeting Mrs Sophia Croft, Anne is hoping she will see Captain Wentworth once again.

Mrs Clay, a widow and lower-class family friend, accompanies Sir Walter and Elizabeth to Bath while Anne decides to stay with Charles Musgrove and her sister Mary for a couple of months at Uppercross Cottage. Mary is prone to complaining and Anne finds herself listening sympathetically to her sister's woes. In fact, Charles Musgrove would have preferred to marry Anne (she refused him because of her continued love for Wentworth), but he remains patient with his wife's problems.

Anne becomes involved with Charles's family and here she enjoys the company of Mr and Mrs Musgrove and their daughters, Henrietta and Louisa. The Musgroves' home at Uppercross is a busy and loving household. The environment is good for Anne, who feels she lacked a loving home with her father and older sister.

Great excitement abounds when news is received that Captain Wentworth, who has just returned from sea, will be visiting his sister at Kellynch Hall. Musgrove and Wentworth soon become friends and the captain becomes a daily visitor at Uppercross, where his manner towards Anne is conciliatory and polite, much to her disappointment. In fact, Wentworth seems rather taken with the Musgrove sisters, Henrietta, and particularly Louisa. Anne is sensible enough to keep her feelings to herself and resigns herself to the fact that she has lost her love for ever.

The family take a trip to Lyme, where Wentworth suggests they visit his friends, the Harvilles. It is here that Anne comes to the attention of a gentleman named Mr Elliot, Anne's cousin and the heir to Kellynch Hall. While out walking one morning on the beach, Louisa Musgrove is knocked unconscious in a fall and it is Anne who remains calm and does all she can for her friend while everyone else believes the young woman to be dead. It is Anne who summons help for the injured Louisa, who although destined to recover, will need to spend some considerable time in Lyme.

Wentworth blames himself for the accident and determines to help the Musgrove family. The accident has tempered Louisa's impetuous nature and she becomes acquainted with Captain James Benwick, a friend of the Harvilles, who is mourning the death of his fiancée and sister of his friend, Fanny Harville. Meanwhile, Anne returns to Uppercross to care for the younger Musgrove children, but after a few weeks leaves to stay with trusted friend Lady Russell.

Some time after the Christmas festivities, Anne and Lady Russell depart for Bath, where they rejoin the Elliot household. Sir Walter and Elizabeth are glad to have Anne to stay, which makes her more comfortable as she was convinced they cared little for her.

Anne is introduced more formally to her cousin, William Elliot, who has by now made peace with his estranged uncle, Sir Walter. The falling-out occurred when Elliot

Left: *Sally Hawkins as Anne Elliot, the protagonist of Persuasion*

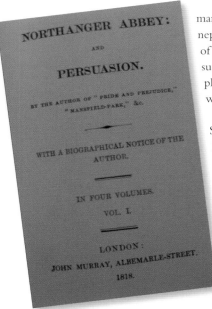

NORTHANGER ABBEY:

AND

PERSUASION.

BY THE AUTHOR OF " PRIDE AND PREJUDICE,"
" MANSFIELD-PARK," &c.

WITH A BIOGRAPHICAL NOTICE OF THE
AUTHOR.

IN FOUR VOLUMES.

VOL. I.

LONDON:
JOHN MURRAY, ALBEMARLE-STREET.

1818.

Above & Right:
*Persuasion was
published in 1818,
after Jane Austen's
death*

married a woman whom Sir Walter deemed unsuitable for his nephew, but William is now a widower. Despite the healing of the family rift, Anne wonders what prompted her cousin to suddenly appear and make his apologies, but she finds Elliot pleasing, although she remains wary of him. Elliot, it seems, wishes Anne to become his wife.

Meanwhile, she has also been reacquainted with Mrs Smith, her old school friend and one-time close friend of Elliot, who has recently been widowed herself. Mrs Smith confides in Anne that Elliot only wants to marry her to ensure that he becomes sole heir to Kellynch Hall. She also warns the protagonist that she was treated badly by Anne's cousin in the past and that Elliot fears Sir Walter will marry Mrs Clay and perhaps have a son, which would end his right to inherit the family estate. Of course, Anne is appalled by this news. Mrs Clay, it is revealed, is in collusion with Elliot.

The Crofts also arrived in Bath and they bring the Elliots some news. Henrietta is engaged to be married to her cousin, Charles Hayter, while Louisa has agreed to marry Captain Benwick, the man she met while convalescing in Lyme. Anne is pleased for her friends and is particularly overjoyed that Captain Wentworth is not one of the betrothed. He, by now exceedingly rich, arrives in Bath.

Sir Walter reluctantly allows Wentworth to join the family's social circle. Wentworth, who has not lost his feelings for Anne – any more than she has lost hers for him – becomes jealous when he believes that Elliot and Anne may be united and he writes his former love a letter in which he pours out his heart. Unsurprisingly, Anne is overjoyed at his declaration of undying love and they soon become engaged.

With the increase in Wentworth's estate, this time both Sir Walter and Lady Russell give the couple their blessing. Elliot is shocked that his plans have been foiled and when he leaves Bath with Mrs Clay the rumours are rife that they are together. This just confirms for Anne that they were in it together all along.

The novel's protagonist, Anne Elliot, is a practical woman who is often overlooked by her father yet remains conscious of her duty to her social position and manages to balance what is expected of her against her own desires. However, with Captain Wentworth having made his own fortune by making his way up the naval ranks, he is deemed unsuitable for Anne by Sir Walter, despite

his kind and gentle nature, his virtue and his good education. As in all Austen novels, Sir Walter is taken on a journey of learning and acceptance and eventually, when Wentworth is proved to be a suitable match for his daughter, he relents and gives his blessing.

Interestingly, at the end of the novel, only Elizabeth Elliot remains unmarried. As a vain woman who places great emphasis on social standing, she has decided that there is no suitor of adequate birth and so prefers to miss out on the happiness of love.

In classic Austen style, some characters have been rewarded for their honest and virtuous approach to life while others have learned a great deal and some have not changed their stance at all. Novels such as *Persuasion* show how clearly perceptive Austen was with regard to human nature and how much she was encouraging society to re-evaluate its perceptions and over-riding principles.

Northanger Abbey (published posthumously, 1818)

This novel was actually the first of Austen's to be ready for publication, even though work on *Sense And Sensibility* and *Pride And Prejudice* had already begun. *Northanger Abbey* was written in 1789, revised for publication in 1803 and sold to Crosbie & Co in London. However, it remained on the publisher's shelves for many years and was eventually sold back to Henry Austen for £10, the same amount for which it was bought. To be fair to Crosbie & Co, they had no idea that the author was Jane Austen, who had already published four popular novels.

It was further revised before being bound with *Persuasion* and published posthumously in late December 1817, although the title page records the date of publication as 1818. It was the first two volumes of what was intended to be a four-volume set. Originally entitled *Susan* after the main character in the novel, *Northanger Abbey* was written at a time of great political turmoil at the turn of the century, when government censorship was rife in the literary world.

When *Susan* was eventually renamed, Austen also chose to change the name of her protagonist to Catherine. Perhaps not as acutely executed in terms of ironic wit and satire as her later novels, *Northanger Abbey* is undoubtedly Austen in its approach, and the irony is often exaggerated and almost sarcastic. It is generally an ironic parody of Gothic novels – popular at the time when Jane was writing – and the new and upcoming light romances that were gaining in momentum despite their unsophisticated approach.

Northanger Abbey is the story of young Catherine Morland, who is coming of age. The novel is divided into two sections: Book I and Book II. The books are significantly different in both setting and tone.

In Book I, the Allen family, who are friends of the Morlands, offer to take Catherine with them to Bath, where wealthier members of British society abide. An eager, 17-year-old Catherine accepts the invitation, leaving her relatively sheltered life for an

Left: *Scene from a television adaption of Northanger Abbey, 2007*

exciting new world. Here she meets Henry Tilney, a young clergyman who impresses the youngster with his wit and conversation and she quickly falls for him, despite not seeing him again for some time after their initial meeting.

Mrs Thorpe, an old acquaintance of Mrs Allen, has three daughters. Isabella Thorpe

is slightly older than Catherine and introduces her new friend to the social circles in Bath where they attend balls and dances and indulge in fashion and gossip. Both the girls' brothers, James Morland and John Thorpe, then come to the city – the two men were friends at Oxford University – and Isabella wastes no time in making her feelings for James Morland obvious through her flirtatious advances. The couple fall in love and everyone is aware of it except Catherine.

John Thorpe, in turn, attempts to woo Catherine, but a chance meeting at a dance with Henry Tilney puts paid to his romantic ambitions. Isabella is no longer much available as a companion for Catherine and she turns to Eleanor Tilney, Henry's sister, for friendship. Eleanor establishes in her own mind that her new friend has feelings for Henry but keeps her thoughts to herself.

When rain washes away Catherine's chances of taking a walk with Eleanor and Henry, she finds herself pressured into riding with John Thorpe. During the ride she spots the brother and sister heading for her house for the planned walk, but John angers Catherine when he refuses to let her stop and inform her friends that she is unavailable.

She is able later to apologise to them and the three make plans for another walk. But, once again, John, James and Isabella interrupt their plans and pressure her into another outing. This time Catherine refuses and takes her longed-for walk with Henry and his sister around Beechen Cliff.

Catherine is pleased when she discovers that both Eleanor and Henry share her love

Left: *Felicity
Jones played
Catherine Morland
in ITV's 2007
adaptation of
Northanger Abbey*

of books and novels. She returns home later to find her brother has become engaged to Isabella Thorpe. She briefly meets with John Thorpe, who is leaving Bath for a short period; unbeknown to Catherine, however, he believes that she is in love with him.

The second book begins with the arrival of Captain Frederick Tilney, older brother of Henry and Eleanor. He and Isabella (who by now is not impressed with James Morland's modest income) begin a dangerous flirtation while Eleanor invites Catherine to her family home in Northanger Abbey. General Tilney, Eleanor's father, is also pleased to invite his daughter's young friend to his home and Catherine, once again, eagerly accepts the invitation. She is particularly taken with the idea of visiting a real abbey and hoping to see more of Henry, but before she leaves, Isabella informs her that John is intending to propose. Catherine asks her friend to write to her brother and apologise on her behalf that any proposal from John would be refused.

Frederick Tilney and Isabella then openly flirt in front of Catherine, who is appalled by their behaviour. She immediately asks Henry to make sure that Frederick leaves Isabella alone for the sake of her relationship with James, but Henry refuses. He is well aware that Isabella is just as guilty as Frederick but hopes that the news that his brother's regiment will be leaving Bath shortly will be enough to placate Catherine.

The protagonist is so intrigued by Northanger Abbey on her journey there that she tells Henry what she imagines it will be like. She concludes that it will resemble the haunted ruins of the Gothic novels she loves, and Henry is so amused at her thoughts that he tells Catherine about how her first night there might be, in a hypothetical account that includes storms, secret passages and mysterious goings-on. By comparison, the abbey turns out to duller than Catherine expected and all her frightening ideas are abruptly shattered. In fact, disappointingly for Catherine, the abbey is a normal family home.

While at the abbey, with an overactive imagination, Catherine becomes intrigued with the death of General Tilney's wife some years before. With her mind on Gothic plots, she even imagines that the General murdered his wife, and she sneaks into Mrs Tilney's old quarters where, unsurprisingly, she discovers absolutely nothing out of the ordinary. But Catherine is caught by Henry, who guesses her motives for being in his mother's old room. He shames his house guest, who immediately resumes her moralistic behaviour in order to win back his approval.

James Morland writes to Catherine to inform her that his engagement to Isabella has been called off and she immediately blames Frederick for the break-up. However, Henry

tells her of Isabella's part in proceedings and she becomes convinced of her friend's guilt. Henry takes Catherine to visit his house at Woodston and the General begins to hint at marriage between the young couple.

A second letter arrives for Catherine. This time it's from Isabella, asking her to apologise to James on her behalf. It seems that Frederick Tilney has left her. Understandably, Catherine is offended and angry that Isabella is trying to manipulate her.

Henry leaves for his house in Woodston and the General travels away on business. But he returns unexpectedly and demands that Eleanor send Catherine away from Northanger Abbey the following day. Although embarrassed, Eleanor carries out her father's wishes and Catherine has no choice but to return to Fullerton, her family home.

As glad as her family are to see Catherine, they are annoyed by General Tilney's rude treatment of their daughter and she, in turn, becomes depressed. However, Henry suddenly arrives at Fullerton and proposes to Catherine, explaining that John Thorpe was the man behind his father's sudden dismissal of her. John had told the General that

Catherine was from a wealthy family (at the time when he thought she loved him), but he became bitter when he learned that she did not in fact love him and spitefully told General Tilney that the Morlands were virtually impoverished. Eleanor's father was devastated by Thorpe's news, but was in a more jovial mood when his daughter married a wealthy man soon after. Once he is correctly informed that the Morlands have a modest income, he relents and consents to the marriage of Henry and Catherine.

Several Gothic novels, including two by neo-classical author Anne Radcliffe: *The Mysteries Of Udolpho* and *The Italian*, are mentioned in *Northanger Abbey*. Austen uses satire to bring the earlier novelists' books into her own and repeats this exercise with Regina Maria Roche's *Clermont*. When later research revealed that these novels actually did exist, there was a move to publish them despite the fact that Austen had parodied them. Austen's biographer, Claire Tomalin, has suggested that Jane intended this light-hearted parody, containing references to well-known literature of the time, as entertainment to be enjoyed by her family.

Juvenilia, short stories and unfinished novels

Interestingly, Austen was exploring her chosen subject matter right from the start of her writing career. *The Three Sisters,* written around 1792, is in the form of a short epistolary novel – meaning the story is told through a series of letters written by the main characters – in much the same way as Samuel Richardson's *Pamela.* Even though it is early Austen, the novel already contains much of the irony that was to become her trademark and implicitly criticises the expectation that women could only progress in life if they climbed the social ladder through marriage. Despite the fact that Austen's juvenilia and later novels all explore this theme, she herself didn't believe that women should have to marry in order to leave the parental home or save themselves from poverty.

What seems incredible about Austen's insight is that she was just 17 when she wrote *The Three Sisters* and was just coming of marrying age herself. In the short novel, it is the character of Sophie who represents Austen's own views and not Mary, who is shown to have a weak disposition and who makes an inappropriate decision, which the author harshly exposes. However, Austen is careful not to minimise the pressures that women were facing at the time.

Other juvenilia include *Love And Freindship* with its famous misspelling, *History Of England, Catherine, Jack And Alice, Frederic And Elfrida* and *The Beautiful Cassandra,* which was one of the funniest works Austin ever wrote, has as its subject her sister Cassandra and is dedicated (with permission) to her lifelong companion and confidante.

Besides the short works, Austen also wrote three unfinished novels. *The Watsons* was eventually completed by her niece, Catherine Hubback, but it was probably *Sanditon* that was the most important. Written while she was ill in 1817, the novel is also known as *Sand And Sanditon* and was originally entitled *The Brothers.* Here the author explores her interest in social politics.

In the novel, the residents of Sanditon must create a town within their own social circles. The town is built around the words of the inhabitants and the conversations they have rather than through the practical construction of homes and buildings. Based around the Parker brothers – for whom it was presumably originally named – the novel shows the author's interest in communication; something she had experimented with since her first unfinished work, *Lady Susan*.

Despite the fact that Austen had less than six months to live when she began the novel, it is fresh, innovative and extremely witty, and builds on the theme set out in *Persuasion* that men of lowly birth can, and do, overcome prejudice to acquire the status, through sheer hard work and determination, that puts them squarely in the upper echelons of society.

Many have tried to continue the manuscript in the style of Austen with what they see as her vision. Such authors include Marie Dobbs and Anne Telscombe (suspected pseudonyms either for different people, or perhaps for the same person), DJ Eden and Anna Austen Lefroy, the author's niece, who wrote a version entitled *Jane Austen's Sanditon; A Continuation*.

Lady Susan, written around 1795, shows Austen's epistolary genre at its best and it seems a shame it went unpublished. The short novel begins with the selfish behaviour of Lady Susan, a woman who is resigned to finding a husband for herself and her daughter but who enjoys plenty of dalliances on her quest. The characters are manifested by their actions as a result of the letters they receive while the heroine alters the tone of her own letters depending on the intended recipient. One thing is clear: there are many letters between the female characters that portray feminine gossip and jealousy.

The Watsons, which remained incomplete, was written around 1803 and probably abandoned when Austen's father died in Bath in 1805. The story centres around Mr Watson, a widowed clergyman who is gravely ill at the start of the novel, and who has two sons and four daughters. His youngest child, Emma, has been more fortunate than her siblings and was brought up by a wealthy aunt, who gave her a grounded education and a more genteel environment in which to grow.

When her aunt remarries, Emma finds she has to return to her father's house, where she is astonished by the reckless way in which two of her older sisters are trying to find themselves husbands. Living nearby is the titled Osborne family and Emma soon attracts the attention of young Lord Osborne. Ultimately, she rejects social position, and to some extent duty, when she decides to marry the Osbornes' young tutor.

At least two attempts were made to complete the novel: one during the 19th century by one of Austen's nieces, the other simply written under the name of 'Another Lady'. However, it was Catherine Hubback who eventually completed her aunt's work in the mid 19th century.

Left: *Jane Austen's memorial in Winchester*

Chapter 3

Film and Television

Right: *On the set of the film Sense and Sensibility, 1995*

All six of Jane Austen's major novels have been adapted for the cinema and the television screen, with varying degrees of success, over the decades. Surprisingly, however, film-makers do not seem to have realised the huge potential popularity of Austen movies until well into the era of television.

Sense And Sensibility

The first Austen novel to be published has a long history of screen adaptations, but they didn't start until 1950, when Delbert Mann directed HR Hays' screenplay for an episode of the live dramatic series *The Philco-Goodyear Television Playhouse* on the American TV network NBC. This formula has also proved popular in the US in more recent years: adaptations of *Sense And Sensibility* have appeared as episodes of *Masterpiece Theatre* in 2008 and *HBO First Look* (1995, as a foretaste of what was to come later in the year on the big screen). In addition, the novel has formed the basis of quite a few TV series.

One came in 1971, when the BBC brought out its full period drama armoury for an adaptation written by Denis Constanduros and directed by David Giles. Among the cast were Joanna David as Elinor Dashwood, Ciaran Madden as Marianne Dashwood, Robin Ellis as Edward Ferrars, Clive Francis as John Willoughby and Richard Owens

as Colonel Brandon. The series was warmly received by critics and audiences alike, although it has been noted that the BBC resurrected a floral gown worn by Ciaran Madden for its adaptation of *Emma* in 1972. This would not be the last time the BBC recycled its Austen-period costumes.

The Beeb had another go at *Sense And Sensibility* in 1981, when Rodney Bennett directed a script by Alexander Baron and Denis Constanduros (again) for a seven-episode series. This time the part of Elinor was taken by Irene Richard, Tracey Childs played Marianne and further roles were filled by Bosco Hogan (Ferrars), Peter Woodward (Willoughby) and Robert Swann (Colonel Brandon). This adaptation received slightly fewer plaudits than the 1971 series, although it was hailed as a must for Austen fans.

In 1995, *Sense And Sensibility* was adapted for the big screen by renowned actress Emma Thompson and the Columbia Pictures/Mirage production was directed by Ang Lee. Filmed on location in Devon and Wiltshire – including in the cobbled streets of Plymouth and at Saltram House, Berry Pomeroy and Compton Castle – the adaptation was notable for its faithfulness to the novel.

The film won a number of awards including the Academy Award for Best Adapted Screenplay (Emma Thompson) and the Golden Bear award for Best Film at the Berlin International Film Festival. BAFTA awards included Best Film (Lindsay Doran and Ang Lee), Best Performance by an Actress in a Leading Role (Emma Thompson) and Best Performance by an Actress in a Supporting Role (Kate Winslet). Other members of a star-studded cast included Hugh Grant as Edward Ferrars, Robert Hardy as Sir John Middleton, Alan Rickman as Colonel Brandon, Imelda Staunton as Charlotte Palmer, Imogen Stubbs as Lucy Steele and Hugh Laurie as Mr Palmer.

In 2008 it fell to the BBC again to compare favourably to Ang Lee's 1995 film version. Its three-hour, three-episode adaptation, written by Andrew Davies and directed by John Alexander, starred Hattie Morahan as Elinor, Charity Wakefield as Marianne,

Dan Stevens as Ferrars, Dominic Cooper as Willoughby and David Morrissey as Colonel Brandon. It was indeed highly rated by the critics.

The novel has inspired other films apart from straight adaptations. The Angel Gracia-directed *From Prada To Nada* made its bow in cinemas in 2011 and won an ALMA Award for Alexa Vega, who starred as Mary Dominguez, the younger and more frivolous of two sisters. Another modern-day translation of the novel came the same year in the form of *Scents And Sensibility*, which retained the names of Elinor and Marianne Dashwood. The film, directed by Brian Brough, did not find many fans, however.

There has even been a musical film version of *Sense And Sensibility* in the Tamil language, called *Kandukondain Kandukondain* and released in India in 2000. And as recently as 2013 another musical adaptation, *Sense And Sensibility, The Musical*, was premiered by the Denver Center Theatre Company, but there do not seem to be any plans to film the stage show.

Pride And Prejudice

Left: *Joe Wright poses for photographs after winning the Carl Foreman award for Pride and Prejudice*

Film adaptations of *Pride And Prejudice* began in 1938 with a very early BBC television broadcast produced by Michael Barry. The 55-minute play, of which little is known and nothing seems to remain, was transmitted live and in black and white, of course, and it featured Curigwen Lewis as Elizabeth Bennet and Andrew Osborn as Fitzwilliam Darcy. Further down the cast list may be spied the name of Mervyn Johns, later to star in many an Ealing Studios film.

A stage version of *Pride And Prejudice* was produced in New York in 1935, and it formed the basis of a 1940 film directed by Robert Z Leonard. Greer Garson (Elizabeth Bennet) and Laurence Olivier (Mr Darcy) starred in a film that is remembered as one of the best versions – perhaps *the* best – of Austen's most famous novel. So struck with the production was the *New York Times* that it described the movie as 'the most deliciously pert comedy of old manners, the most crisp and crackling satire in costume that we in this corner can remember ever having seen on the screen'. The film is set in a later period than the novel, for the simple reason that Metro-Goldwyn-Mayer wanted to flaunt some more elaborate costumes than those worn by the women of Austen's time.

The novel was adapted for numerous TV mini-series before Fay Weldon wrote the screenplay for a BBC series broadcast in 1980. Directed by Cyril Coke, it starred Elizabeth Garvie as Elizabeth and David Rintoul as Mr Darcy and was broadcast on PBS in the USA. It was well received, although some internet-based critics couldn't help pointing out that the BBC was up to its costume-recycling tricks again.

Guess who produced a six-episode TV series of *Pride And Prejudice* in 1995? No prizes – yes, it was the BBC. This adaptation was memorable for the appearance of Colin Firth as Mr Darcy and Jennifer Ehle as Elizabeth Bennet, and was directed by Simon Langton from a script by Andrew Davies. The public's reaction was overwhelmingly positive, and among the awards the adaptation received were a BAFTA (Best Actress)

and a Primetime Emmy (Outstanding Costume Design).

More awards came the way of Joe Wright's 2005 film starring Keira Knightley as Elizabeth Bennet, Matthew Macfadyen, Brenda Blethyn and Donald Sutherland. Based on a screenplay by Deborah Moggach, the Working Title/Studio Canal film was filmed on location around the UK, including the stately Chatsworth House in Derbyshire and Wilton House in Salisbury, which was used to represent Pemberley. Groombridge Place in Kent was used as a location for Longbourn while Basildon Park in Berkshire represented Netherfield Park. Burghley, near Stamford, and the Lincolnshire town itself, were also used during filming. Dame Judi Dench and Penelope Wilton also starred in this brilliant adaptation.

As is often the case when a large work of literature is adapted into around two hours of film, there were plenty of differences between the film and the original story. For instance, in Wright's film, several supporting characters were eliminated from the screenplay and the crisis endured by the Bennet family when Lydia elopes with Wickham was compressed.

The story of Pride And Prejudice has been the base from which many a film-maker has produced looser adaptations. One of these was Bridget Jones' Diary (2001), in which Colin Firth (Mr Darcy in the BBC TV production of 1995) played the character of Mark Darcy – no coincidence there. Pride & Prejudice – A Latter-Day Comedy (2003) was a modern-day adaptation set among a Mormon community in Utah and Bride And Prejudice (2004) was a Bollywood reading of the story directed by Gurinder Chadha. Detective novel author P.D. James's murder mystery set six years after Elizabeth and Darcy's marriage, entitled Death Comes to Pemberley, was also made into a TV mini-series in 2013.

Mansfield Park

The BBC first got to grips with Austen's *Mansfield Park* in 1983, when David Giles directed a six-episode series based on Kenneth Taylor's screenplay. Sylvestra Le Touzel starred as Fanny Price, Christopher Villiers as Tom Bertram and Nicholas Farrell as Edmund Bertram and the production featured a host of familiar names. Filming took place at the Brympton d'Evercy manor house near Yeovil in Somerset and at Somerley House in the New Forest, Hampshire.

In 1999, the UK film *Mansfield Park* was released by BBC Films in association with HAL Films. It was written and directed by Patricia Rozema, and most of the film was shot on location at Kirby Hall in Northamptonshire. It was a loose adaptation of the novel, for the life of Jane Austen was introduced into the film, and it also differed from the book in its treatment of the issue of slavery.

Starring Frances O'Connor and Jonny Lee Miller, the film also featured Harold Pinter as Sir Thomas Bertram, Lindsay Duncan as Lady Bertram/Mrs Price, Sheila Gish and Hannah Taylor Gordon as the young Fanny Price. Rozema's film divided the critics sharply, with many preferring the 1983 adaptation but others praising its individuality.

In 2007 ITV broadcast a two-hour small-screen adaptation of *Mansfield Park* starring Billie Piper as Fanny Price. Written by Maggie Wadey and directed by Iain B MacDonald, it received plenty of criticism for not staying true to Austen's original work and for the standard of the production. Filming locations included Newby Hall in North Yorkshire.

A loose adaptation of *Mansfield Park* set in modern-day New York was released in 1990 under the title of *Metropolitan*. Written and directed by Whit Stillman, it received an Oscar nomination in the Best Original Screenplay category.

Emma

Emma has proved as popular as any of Jane Austen's novels among broadcasters and film-makers. The history of adaptations began in 1948, when the BBC broadcast a live version written and starring Judy Campbell and directed by Michael Barry. The American network NBC got in on the act with live broadcasts in 1954 and 1957 and then it was back to the BBC, which ran a six-part series in 1960. This adaptation starred Diana Fairfax as Emma and was directed by Campbell Logan. The US broadcaster CBS produced a version, transmitted live, the same year.

Twelve years were to go by before the BBC attempted another *Emma*, releasing its six-part series in 1972. Written by Denis Constanduros

and directed by John Glenister, it starred Doran Goodwin as Emma Woodhouse and John Carson as Mr Knightley, and was hailed in some quarters as the best screen adaptation up to that point.

An Oscar-winning *Emma* was released in 1996 by Matchmaker Films and Haft Entertainment, starring Gwyneth Paltrow in the leading role. Directed by Douglas McGrath and also starring Jeremy Northam, Toni Collette, Greta Scacchi, Juliet Stevenson and Ewan McGregor, the film gained rave reviews while Paltrow won critical acclaim for her portrayal of Emma. Comic scenes were provided by Alan Cumming and Juliet Stevenson as Mr and Mrs Elton while real-life mother and daughter Phyllida Law and Sophie Thompson played the roles of Mrs Bates and Miss Bates. Rachel Portman's music won the Oscar for Best Original Score.

However, McGrath's film faced competition from a ITV television movie that was released the same year. Adapted by Andrew Davies and directed by Diarmuid Lawrence, the film also won plenty of praise and went on to receive two Emmys. Starring Kate Beckinsale as Emma, Mark Strong as Mr Knightley and Prunella Scales as Miss Bates, it was felt by many critics that this version was truer to Austen's original work, and that the screenplay was superior to the more glamorous film version.

Most critics agreed that Paltrow and Beckinsale were both well cast as Emma, but the superb production of the TV version just tipped the balance for some. The fact that the productions came out at the roughly the same time caused some confusion, and, whereas Sophie Thompson's interpretation of Miss Bates in the film version was judged outstanding by many critics, there was a consensus that the casting of Prunella Scales in the same role for the ITV version was a little odd, even though the actress gave a great performance.

The BBC came up with yet another adaptation in 2009, when Romola Garai played Emma in a four-episode series written by Sandy Welch and directed by Jim O'Hanlon. This was another plaudit-gathering version of the novel, with Jonny Lee Miller in the

role of Mr Knightley and Michael Gambon playing Emma's father. It was filmed in various locations in Kent, Surrey, Sussex and London.

Clueless (1995) was a humorous modernisation of the novel directed by Amy Heckerling and starring Alicia Silverstone. Well received by critics and public, it in turn inspired *Aisha*, a Hindi-language version of the film set in Delhi.

Above: *Setting up for filming of ITV's 2007 adaptation of Persuasion*

Persuasion

The first screen attempt at *Persuasion* came in 1960 from, naturally, the BBC. This adaptation was written by Barbara Burnham and Michael Voysey and directed by Campbell Logan but, sadly, all four episodes are believed to be lost. Daphne Slater played Anne Elliot and Paul Daneman took the role of Captain Wentworth. Next time out, in 1971, the BBC managed to hang on to its copies. Julian Mitchell wrote the screenplay and Howard Baker directed Ann Firbank (Anne Elliot) and Bryan Marshall (Captain Wentworth) in a series that was broadcast in five episodes.

Twenty-four years later, the BBC released a television film version starring Amanda Root as Anne Elliot and Ciaran Hinds as Captain Wentworth. Other cast members included Susan Fleetwood as Lady Russell, Corin Redgrave as Sir Walter Elliot and Fiona Shaw as Mrs Croft. Samuel West took the role of estranged nephew William

Elliot, while Sophie Thompson was a convincing Mary Musgrove. Elizabeth Elliot was played by Phoebe Nicholls and the adaptation was directed by Roger Michell with a screenplay by Nick Dear. The film was a resounding success and won BAFTA awards for Best Single Drama, Best Photography and Lighting, Best Costume Design, Best Design and Best Original Television Music.

It was followed in 2007 by another television adaptation, this time by ITV, starring Sally Hawkins, Rupert Penry-Jones, Alice Krige, Anthony Head, Julia Davis and Mary Stockley. Directed by Adrian Shergold and adapted by Simon Burke, the production wasn't deemed to have reached the dizzy heights of its predecessor, although Tobias Menzies, who played William Elliot, received rave reviews.

Northanger Abbey

The first of Jane Austen's novels was adapted for the small screen in 1986 by A&E Network and the BBC. Directed by Giles Foster with a screenplay by Maggie Wadey, the cast included Katharine Schlesinger as Catherine and Peter Firth as Henry Tilney. Supporting roles were filled by Robert Hardy (General Tilney), Googie Withers (Mrs Allen), Cassie Stuart (Isabella Thorpe), Jonathan Coy (John Thorpe), Philip Bird (James Morland), Ingrid Lacey (Eleanor Tilney) and Greg Hicks (Frederick Tilney).

Granada Productions and WGBH Boston called on the prodigious writing talents of Andrew Davies and the direction of Jon Jones for their 2007 film adaptation of *Northanger Abbey*. Felicity Jones starred as Catherine Morland and JJ Field played her love interest, Henry Tilney, in a film screened as part of an ITV Jane Austen season. Shot on location in Ireland, it also featured the voice of Geraldine James as Jane Austen herself, Sylvestra Le Touzel, Carey Mulligan, William Beck and Hugh O'Conor, and *The Guardian* called it 'the perfect Sunday evening blend of eruditeness and pretty frocks'.

Chapter 4

Celebrating Jane Austen

The Jane Austen's House Museum is based in Austen's former home at Chawton – the house in which she wrote some of her best works which is preserved for her fans from the world over. Open at various times all year round, the house is where the author wrote *Mansfield Park*, *Emma* and *Persuasion* and revised *Pride And Prejudice*, *Sense And Sensibility* and *Northanger Abbey*.

Bought by T Edward Carpenter in 1947 with additional funding from the Jane Austen Society, the house was turned into an independent charity administered by the Jane Austen Memorial Trust. The trust aims to preserve the museum for the nation, to acquire, catalogue and conserve artefacts and interpret Austen's life for visitors.

It was at Chawton that Austen spent the last eight years of her life. The 17th century house, which retains the charm of a family home, tells the story of Austen and her family through its rooms, exhibition and artefacts. A reference library includes various editions of Austen's published novels, books to help those who wish to study the author in greater depth and a collection of translations of Austen titles.

Not surprisingly, 2013 – the 200th anniversary of the publication of Pride And Prejudice – saw much activity at Chawton commemorating one of literature's most notable events. An exhibition explored the story of the novel and its creation and what it means today while there were also readings of a new dramatic version of the novel and an exhibition of works of art inspired by Pride And Prejudice. On December 16

admission to the museum was free as visitors were invited to celebrate Austen's birthday. For further information call 01420 832262 or visit jane-austens-house-museum.org.uk

The Jane Austen Centre, based in a Georgian house in the centre of Bath, is much more than a visitor attraction in the city where the author once lived. The website features more than 500 articles, a gift shop, information about the Jane Austen Festival, a quiz, the *Jane Austen's Regency World* magazine and a monthly e-newsletter. A permanent exhibition at the centre tells the story of the author's experiences in Bath and the influences the city had on her writings. Also on offer are lectures and walking tours that take visitors to the houses where Austen lived plus the settings for *Northanger Abbey* and *Persuasion*.

In an interesting if somewhat cheeky experiment, *Jane Austen's Regency World* decided to send sample chapters of *Pride And Prejudice, Northanger Abbey* and *Persuasion* to 18 publishing houses and literary agents to see how an Austen novel would fare in

today's cut-throat publishing environment: not very well, as it turns out. Sent with a synopsis and the biographical details of 'Alison Laydee' – a pun on 'A Lady', the name under which Austen published her novels – the chapters were rejected by all but one recipient, who recognised that the sample manuscripts were possibly by Austen. As *Pride And Prejudice* has been voted the 'number one book that the British nation could

Right: *The Jane Austen Centre, Bath*

not live without' it seems sad that major publishers couldn't recognise a masterpiece when they saw one or didn't realise the significance of what they had received.

The Jane Austen Festival is held in Bath every autumn with walking tours, lectures and workshops on manners and etiquette, among many other activities. For further information contact The Jane Austen Centre on 01225 443000 or visit janeausten.co.uk.

There are many Jane Austen Societies throughout the world. The UK society was founded in 1940 to help secure the cottage at Chawton where Austen spent her last days, and aims to promote Austen and interest in her life and works. At the society's annual general meeting at Chawton, speakers give addresses that are then published in the annual report, in which there are also historical notes and articles, an annual bibliography of Austen books, articles and book reviews. The society consists of regional groups in Bath and Bristol, Cambridge, Hampshire, Kent, London, the Midlands, Norfolk and the Isle of Wight.

The Jane Austen Society of Australia prides itself on not being stuffy, and invites scholars, amateurs, professionals and enthusiasts to gather to study and appreciate Austen's genius. The society is interested in her life and times as well as her works, and believes that Austen's environment contributed greatly to her writing. Meetings take place every two months and conferences and workshops are also held regularly. The society has groups in Sidney, Melbourne and Adelaide.

The Jane Austen Society of North America's mission is to foster the study, appreciation and understanding of Austen's works, life, times and genius. It provides benefits for its members through grants, has an annual journal (*Persuasion*) publishes a newsletter and offers members the opportunity to participate in regional groups. The society holds an annual meeting in a different location each year and prides itself on providing a 'fun' environment – it is keen to emphasise that Austen was a comic writer. The society was founded by Canadian-born Joan Austen-Leigh, the great-great-great niece of the novelist, and Jack Grey from New York, and came

Right: *Bath Abbey, an example of the stunning architecture to be found in Bath*

Left:
*Screenwriters
and actors at
the Jane Austen
Masterpiece
Theatre*

about when the two met at Chawton in 1975. Today, the society has more than 4,500 members.

The Jane Austen Society of Buenos Aires is the only society in South America and is proud of that fact. During its first three years, all members of the society re-read the six major novels and the three unfinished titles. The society was founded by Patrick Orpen Dudgeon in 1997.

There are also Jane Austen Societies in Scandinavia, central Africa, Malaysia and the Netherlands. Despite the fact that Austen is well read in Asia, however, there are no societies in that continent that celebrate her life and works.

With her shrewd understanding of the human mind and ironic wit, it is little wonder that Jane Austen is so admired and revered for her works, which resonate just as strongly with readers today as they did in the early 19th century.

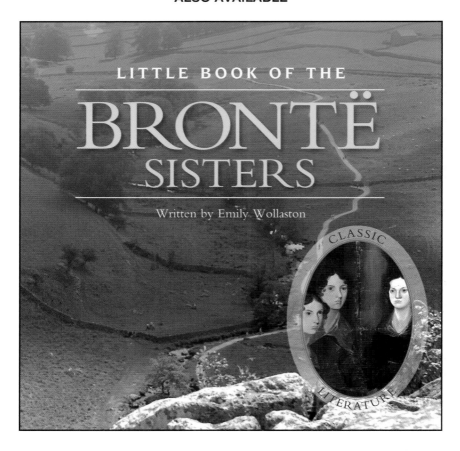

LITTLE BOOK OF THE

BRONTË
SISTERS

Written by Emily Wollaston

CLASSIC

LITERATURE

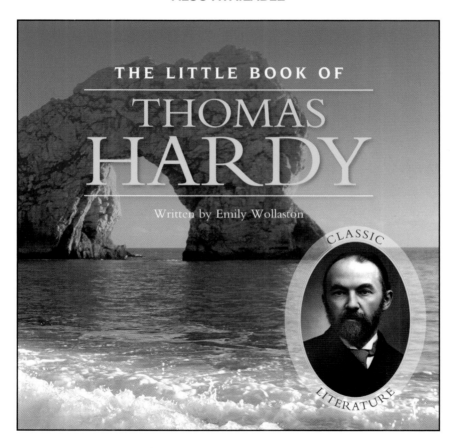

THE LITTLE BOOK OF

THOMAS HARDY

Written by Emily Wollaston

CLASSIC LITERATURE

The pictures in this book were provided courtesy of the following:

GETTY IMAGES
101 Bayham Street, London NW1 0AG

SHUTTERSTOCK
www.shutterstock.com

WIKICOMMONS
commons.wikimedia.org

Design & Artwork by Scott Giarnese

Published by G2 Entertainment Limited

Publishers: Jules Gammond & Edward Adams

Written by Emily Wollaston